# Live
# By The
# Spirit

## Inspired Thoughts
## Volume 1

Kathleen E. Walls, Psy.D.

I give honor, praise, and thanks to the Most High God.

I thank my divine helpers, the ancestors, and those who have guided and helped me along the way.

I dedicate this book to you.

Kathleen E. Walls, Psy.D.

# Contents

*"Since we live by the Spirit,*

*Let us keep in step with the Spirit."*

Galatians 5:25


God,

Thank You for the insight, revelations, and wisdom that
You have given to me and enabled me to share with others.

May these inspired thoughts be a blessing, benefit,

and guide for others.

Amen.

Kathleen E. Walls, Psy.D.

# INTRODUCTION

I was led to share *Live By the Spirit, Inspired Thoughts*, to help people do just that ... live by the Spirit. When I refer to Spirit, I refer to the essence within and around us that connects us to the One Most High, the One Supreme God. This essence helps us to live as our highest divine self and thus, in turn, live our G.R.E.A.T.E.S.T. Life! Through prayer, meditation, being still, and listening to that still, small voice, we are given guidance which enables us to live by the Spirit.

Through the years I have learned to follow this guiding voice because it always leads me exactly where I want to go and/or where I need to be. By living my life this way, I understand the difficulties and challenges, as well as the joys and benefits, of life events. I recognize that the difficulties and challenges act as tools to wean and prune aspects of myself that are not helping me live and function as my highest divine self, and are no longer necessary. I am a person who looks at life as if it is a school; therefore I seek to know and recognize the lessons that are learned from interactions, the skills that have been accumulated and strengthened, and the areas that still need to develop and strengthen.

I believe we are all given Spirit-led guidance throughout our lives. As we learn to and commit to living by the Spirit, we begin to recognize that this guidance comes in many ways, such as through inner knowing and dreams, in moments of inspiration, as well as through other people, books, media, and nature. Another way to say it is that we are learning our personal Spirit language that leads and guides us. Once we get in tune with who we are and learn the signs, symbols, and patterns of our lives, we are able to successfully navigate the roads that lead to living our G.R.E.A.T.E.S.T. Life!

## 1. THE GREATEST GIFT

It is in our relationship with God that we have the **Greatest Gift**. As we open ourselves up to the gift of the relationship, we open ourselves to experience an Ephesians 3:20 life:

"Now all glory to God, who is able, through his mighty power at work within us, to accomplish infinitely more than we might ask or think."

One day I received a quote by Joseph Campbell, via email. The quote stated: "We must be willing to get rid of the life we've planned, so as to have the life that is waiting for us." A few hours later, I checked my horoscope and it ended with: "Don't hold on to your previous expectations. Open your mind and let the unfolding changes show you what's ahead."

So the **Greatest Gift** that I give you is the reminder to open yourself up and allow God to guide you to have a life better than you could ever think or imagine.

God bless, and live by the Spirit!

What inspired thoughts emerged during/after this reading?

## 2. WHEN SPIRIT SPEAKS

As we look to make changes, accomplish goals, and/or seek direction in life, it is important to be still and listen. By sitting still and becoming clearer on your goals and direction in life, guidance will come to you so that these goals are achieved.

Many times we pray and ask for guidance and direction in life, but forget to be still and listen for the answers we seek. My mother used to say, "When your mouth is open, your ears are closed; therefore, if you close your mouth, your ears will open." Psalms 46:10 says, "Be still, and know that I am God" (NLT). As you live by the Spirit, you are partnering with something greater than yourself, to live a life greater than you could ever think or imagine (Ephesians 3:20, paraphrased).

When we hear, we perceive a sound, but *when we listen, we give our attention, wait attentively, and/or follow the directions*.

In A Course in Miracles, Lesson 49 reminds us **"God's Voice speaks to me all through the day."** We have to learn how to discern the voice of Spirit from our own internal and external chatter. As we practice listening to Spirit, we are able to discern and heed Divine direction. Many times, people have good intentions for us, but it is important to remember that Spirit has the Greatest intentions for us. So the question is, "Do you want good, better, or the Greatest?" It really is up to you. The choice is yours!

If you have decided on having the Greatest for yourself, then I encourage you to practice being still and listening, so that you can learn to live and be led by the Spirit. Just as with most skills in life, being still and listening are skills that need practice and will become stronger over time. Some have found it helpful to pray, meditate, listen to music, or journal. Take a few minutes right now and ask Spirit to speak to you. In the stillness of the moment, you may be led to call someone, your phone may ring, you may remember something long forgotten, or you may receive an email or text with the answer that you seek or a message that you need.

As you open yourself to guidance, remember it will come in many forms and from many directions (such as TV, radio, nature, conversations, etc.). Opportunities and possibilities will seem to come out of nowhere, chance meetings that we call coincidences will happen more frequently, and ideas will pop right into your mind.

I encourage you to take a few moments each day, throughout the day, to be still and listen. When you are stuck, confused, or unsure, be still and allow Spirit to guide and direct you. At first, it may seem awkward and you may feel silly, but with practice this regular "personal time out" (PTO) will become a natural part of your life experience.

God bless, and live by the Spirit!

What inspired thoughts emerged during/after this reading?

## 3. SPIRIT LANGUAGE

When we live by the Spirit, we have chosen to partner with something Greater than our physical selves. When we think of the Spirit, we often think of something that is not physical, something that cannot be contained, and something that does not have physical limitations. Take a moment and think about the endless possibilities of partnering with something that is limitless, boundless, and is not constricted or restricted by time or space.

Ask Spirit to speak to you. Know that Spirit speaks in a variety of ways. Some people say they hear a still, small voice inside of them; others say they feel a push or an urge to do something. Give yourself time to sit still, listen, and move to the inner guidance that is speaking to you. This guidance and direction may come to you in a dream, when watching or listening to a television or radio show, while spending time in nature, or during an unexpected conversation. Once you activate and partner with Spirit, your guidance and direction will come in many forms, so be ready!

God bless, and live by the Spirit!

What inspired thoughts emerged during/after this reading?

## 4. PARTNERING WITH SPIRIT

A partner refers to someone with whom you have a common interest, someone who is an ally, a companion. We often think of partnering around the idea of marriage, romantic relationships, or even business relationships. We recognize that during this partnership we are getting to know someone, their likes and dislikes, their expectations, and their hopes and dreams. During this relationship building, we are sharing information about ourselves as well as listening to what is being said, and determining whether or not this would be the best partnership for us.

In the development of a healthy partnership, we are asking ourselves:

1. What will I learn from this partnership?

2. How will I grow in this partnership?

3. What do I bring to this partnership?

4. How are we better/healthier together?

During the development and growth of a healthy partnership, we are looking at how we are changing and transforming for the better. If this is not the case, then it is time to stop and reevaluate the relationship. In one of my favorite movies, *Tombstone*, Doc Holliday has a change of heart and purpose in life and, in one particular scene, he turns to his partner (who hasn't changed her ways) and says, "We must redefine the nature of our association." Doc recognizes that although he had chosen a relationship at one time (that was unhealthy), he has the ability and the courage to change his mind, his behaviors, and the relationship. He decides to choose something better for himself, which also leads to an improvement in other relationships and the community at large.

Relationships require active participation from all parties. Take time to get acquainted with Spirit. You may be led to spend some time alone, meditate, journal, read spiritual books, go to the movies, go out to dinner, or even just settle in for a cozy evening. Enjoy partnering with Spirit.

God bless, and live by the Spirit!

What inspired thoughts emerged during/after this reading?

Kathleen E. Walls, Psy.D.

## 5. GROWING PAINS TO GROWING GAINS

The word *growing* kept ringing in my mind and I thought about the growth process I have gone through as well as growth processes that I have witnessed in others. I do a lot of work with tweens (children between the ages of eight and twelve), where I talk with them about the changes they are going through and the "growing pains" that they may experience, such as pains in their knees and feet, and pains stemming from changes in their relationships with family and friends.

They are beginning to learn about and experience themselves in a new way, and regardless of how many of them don't want to hear about it and want the puberty / growing process to stop, the changes keep happening. Eventually it becomes evident that growing pains are inevitable. Growing pains are a part of life and happen in every aspect of our lives. However, as we get older we come to realize that through/after growing pains, we experience "growing gains."

As I reflected on my spiritual journey, I thought of times when I, too, didn't want to hear certain things and I wanted the spiritual growing pains to stop. During these times I had (and at times still have) what I refer to as spiritual temper tantrums: those times when you want … what you want … when you want it … but no matter how hard you plead your case, justify that this result must come to pass, and then you top it off with your gold-medal pouting champion performance. Ooooohhh, and don't let Spirit lead you to say and/or do something which you don't want to, don't feel ready to do, or which might go against what the alleged real-you wants to do. Next thing you know, the hands go up ... the ears close ... and that good ol' "I'm not listening, I can't hear you" comes out. And if that weren't enough, the battle really kicks in and I escalate to a full-blown spiritual temper tantrum wherein—yes, it happens—I basically say, "Talk to the hand 'cause I am not trying to understand!"

By then, I'm tired. I have worn myself out. And in that quiet moment, when my internal torrent has calmed, the Spirit speaks. The comfort of Spirit's voice takes over, the understanding is given, and the breakthrough occurs. I have moved from *growing pains to growing gains*. I have gained a deeper understanding of how Spirit works in my life. I have gained a deeper understanding of where I still need to grow up. I have gained a deeper understanding of where I still need to be pruned. I have gained a deeper understanding of patience, acceptance, and tolerance of self, which in turn teaches me to have the same for others. Just as with the tweens, I have gained a deeper understanding of myself, thus providing me with an opportunity to experience others and myself in a new way. I have gained a deeper understanding of myself versus the alleged self. Overall, I have gained a deeper understanding of unconditional Divine Love ... a deeper understanding of Spirit.

God bless, and live by the Spirit!

What inspired thoughts emerged during/after this reading?

## 6. GROWING INTO GREATNESS

I thought about the first line on the first page of my book, *The G.R.E.A.T.E.S.T. Soul Journey* (2009), which states, "Humanity is the starting point on the way to Divinity." I thought about the journey of moving from humanity to Divinity. I thought about Jesus' journey in human form. I thought about the building of the relationship between our human self and our Spirit self. And then I heard … "When I was a child, I spoke and thought and reasoned as a child. But when I grew up, I put away childish things" (1 Corinthians 13:11). Selah. The message now seemed so clear. It is as if as a child I thought God was outside of me, but now that I am grown I know that God and I are one! I thought about how God is often represented by capital letters, with an uppercase *G*, as if it represents being grown, versus a lowercase *g*, indicating that the person still needs to grow up.

Needless to say, I quickly looked up the rest of the Scripture, 1 Corinthians 13:12, which states:

> "Now we see things imperfectly as in a cloudy mirror, but then we will see everything with perfect clarity. All that I know now is partial and incomplete, but then I will know everything completely, just as God now knows me completely."

The messages resounded:

- God and I are one

- Humanity *is* the starting point on the way to Divinity

It is as if we enter this matrix of humanity and forget who we are; however, we are given reminders, messages, and messengers along the way to reawaken us to who we really are. Many have said that we are "spirits having a human experience." Ed "Umoja" Herman has said, "We are spiritual beings having a human experience, and we should never allow our human experience to limit our Spiritual Greatness; so embrace and reveal our Spiritual Greatness so God's love for humanity will be seen by all!"

It is during this human experience, this human journey, that we strengthen our relationship with God. As we grow into God, we grow into our Greatness.

God bless, and live by the Spirit!

What inspired thoughts emerged during/after this reading?

## 7. JUST THE TWO OF US

We often think of intimacy as a word that is associated with a physical connection between two people. However, the concept of intimacy is much deeper than just a physical connection. Intimacy is defined as closeness and/or belongingness between people. My definition of intimacy is

$$\text{Trust} + \text{Vulnerability} = \text{Intimacy}$$

Oh boy, *trust* and *vulnerability*, two concepts that often make people feel uncomfortable and lead them to do things to protect themselves ... to pull away instead of draw closer together. Yet there is something so deep and so special about relationships that allow you to be vulnerable, relationships where you are able to trust that the other person will not hurt you or take advantage of you. Trust and vulnerability are essential elements that lead to the Greatest friendships and the Greatest loves.

My relationship with Spirit has always been private. Honestly, it has been my most intimate relationship, one that only a few have been privy to knowing and partially witnessing. Just as in my human-to-human relationships, my spirit-to-Spirit relationship has had many moments when I have felt vulnerable and questioned my ability to trust what Spirit was leading me to say and/or do. It has been through these times that I have had opportunities to strengthen my faith and my/our overall relationship.

Over the years, Spirit has led me to be in contact with more people, and to share more about my relationship with Spirit. I have allowed others to share in that intimate space. As I have and am growing with Spirit, I have been asked to increase my level of *trust* and *vulnerability* by sharing my thoughts, experiences, and beliefs, as well as the ways in which Spirit and I have worked and continue to work together. However, like in any relationship, there is a side, a level of intimacy, that remains private and is between "just the two of us."

As I continue to grow with Spirit, I am being asked to do and share more, and am being placed in what I previously would have called a vulnerable position. Yet, because I trust Spirit, I know I can and will move into a place of strength, a place of assuredness, a place of confidence, and a place of safety. Thus I know that Spirit has my best interest at heart, and I inevitably put my life in Spirit's "hands."

I encourage you to strengthen the intimate connection between you and Spirit.

God bless, and live by the Spirit!

What inspired thoughts emerged during/after this reading?

## 8. BE STILL & LISTEN

"Be Still & Listen" resounded in me. As I sat and listened, I was led to look around and see where I was in my life. I took inventory and began to ask myself a series of questions:

1. Is this where I want to be in my life (my job, relationship, etc.)? If not, where do I want to be and how do I get there?

2. How do I feel mentally, physically, spiritually, and emotionally about where I am? Am I in alignment of mind-body-spirit?

3. Who can I turn to for guidance and direction?

4. Who is Spirit speaking through to speak to me?

So I sat. I then looked to Spirit and asked Spirit to speak to me and guide me, as well as those who needed to deliver *the messages*, so that I could continue to live by the Spirit.

As that week passed, the questions were answered one by one. I was led to contact certain people, received emails with clear and timely messages as well as with answers and/or instructions. I also found myself having the same conversation over and over, which was a sign that Spirit was speaking and I needed to listen. I began to look at the "writing on the wall" and to *read* it! As I comprehended the clear messages before me, the struggle within me ceased, the courage within me sprang forth, I did what was needed to make changes, and Divine peace was restored.

I encourage you to take a few moments and answer the above questions. It is important to pay attention to your bodily reactions as you answer each, and clarify what these bodily reactions mean to you and for you. For instance, I noticed that sometimes I experienced tightening in my shoulders, pangs in my stomach, shortness of breath, and headaches—clear signs that I had made or was about to make a decision out of alignment with my Greatest self … that I was about to be person-led instead of Spirit-led. So take a moment, stand in the mirror, so to speak, and pay attention to all the ways that Spirit is speaking to and through you.

God bless, and live by the Spirit!

What inspired thoughts emerged during/after this reading?

## 9. GOING BEYOND WHAT I KNOW & INTO WHO I AM

It seems sometimes as if I am being moved outside of my territory, into an unfamiliar land. I feel as if I am being moved out of my comfort zone. Yet during this journey, I am discovering more of who I am. I am "Going Beyond What I Know & into Who I Am."

At times, I find myself in a period of reflecting on what I know, so that I can stand comfortably and strong while in this new place, this unfamiliar place. Similar to the journey of *Ordinary* in the **Dream Giver** (2004) by Bruce Wilkinson, at times I feel like I am in the wilderness waiting for the next set of directions and/or signs to lead me to my destination. The lessons include learning to be comfortable and patient, and trust the meantime. In other words, learning to trust and be open to Spirit's guidance ... to God's plan for my life.

This phase of the journey reminds me of moving and/or packing for a trip. When I travel or move I pack what I need and leave the rest, knowing that if I need something else I can pick it up along the way. However, sometimes when I travel I am unsure of what I need, so I take only the basics. For me, the main items that I have "packed" for this part of my journey are "being open to and trusting Spirit."

In my book, *The G.R.E.A.T.E.S.T. Soul Journey*, the "E.S.T." stands for ***Encourages Spiritual Transformation***. As I move into my G.R.E.A.T.E.S.T. self, I am open to Spirit and trust the process of spiritual transformation. I am moving beyond what I know. As I express myself more ... the more talents I use ... the more experiences I have ... the more I move into who I am.

As you continue on your life journey, I encourage you to remain open to Spirit and to move beyond what you know.

God bless, and live by the Spirit!

What inspired thoughts emerged during/after this reading?

## 10. CALL OF DUTY

About fourteen years ago I was attending a workshop and heard someone say, "I was 'called' to do ...." Later that same day I heard someone else say, "I was 'called' to do ...." Each time I heard the phrase "I was called" I felt a rumbling inside me, deep within my belly. I couldn't take it anymore, so I leaned to the row in front of me, excused myself, and asked what they meant by "I was called." The people smiled and said, "God is directing me to do something" and "I have a calling." At that moment, I knew that I had a calling too.

Honestly, I knew that something had been stirring in my Spirit for weeks. I had spoken about it and thought about it, but hadn't done anything about it. I now knew it was time. I was "called to duty." I left the workshop, got in my car, and made a call immediately to put the plan in motion. In true Spirit form, everything fell right into place!

In my book, *The G.R.E.A.T.E.S.T. Soul Journey*, I encourage people to be still, reflect, and reconnect/realign with their soul. When we are in alignment with our soul, we are more attuned to and can recognize when we are receiving a "call." (See 1 Samuel 3).

When we receive a call to duty, it is like an internal push or drive that has a positive impact in our lives *and* the lives of others. Remember, when we answer the call, everything and everyone we need to accomplish the task and/or goal will be provided in a Divine way and in Divine time.

God bless, and live by the Spirit!

What inspired thoughts emerged during/after this reading?

## 11. GO WITH THE FLOW

"Go with the Flow" is what resounded in me this morning. Since I have been called to retreat this month, I have been reflecting on my life and thinking about my personal truth, that which I know to be true of and for me. I thought about times when God and I have moved seamlessly and effortlessly as one, and times when I have struggled. I realized that I usually experience struggle when I am going against the current of Spirit, when I am not going with the flow.

For me, going with the flow means being in alignment with Spirit ... knowing that Spirit and I are working together toward my Greatest good. It does not mean that I will not encounter difficulties or challenges; however, when Spirit fortifies me and I am going with the flow, I know that I am with my perfect partner, the One who will help me navigate the "waters of life."

When I am flowing in and with Spirit, I am able to see a possible way around and beyond a situation, as well as know that I am strong enough to withstand a situation. Situations that once would have caused me to shudder, tremble, or even try to avoid, are now seen as manageable and, possibly, not even difficult. There is the *knowing* that I am equipped and that I am going to come out better on the other side of the situation.

In ***Women Who Run with the Wolves*** by Clarissa Pinkola Estés, she states, "All that you are seeking is also seeking you." Therefore when you go with the flow, you know that you are like a magnet, picking up, attracting, and being led to that which you seek and desire. Thus, it is inevitable that you will receive all that you were created to receive ... so remember to go with the flow.

God bless, and live by the Spirit!

What inspired thoughts emerged during/after this reading?

## ABOUT THE AUTHOR

Dr. Kathleen E. Walls is the owner and founder of the G.R.E.A.T.E.S.T. Counseling & Consulting, located in Philadelphia, PA, the author of *The G.R.E.A.T.E.S.T. Soul Journey* (2009), and the host of her Internet radio and YouTube shows, Dr. Walls & Friends. She is a psycho-dynamically trained and systems-oriented doctor of Clinical Psychology. Dr. Walls counsels, consults, coaches, teaches, and delivers interactive seminars and motivational speeches. She researches and develops strategic plans, programs, and curriculums for a wide range of civic, educational, healthcare, and business enterprises. Dr. Walls enjoys traveling domestically and internationally, embracing and facilitating cross-cultural exchanges, incorporating a holistic perspective in the development of leaders, mentoring young people, students, and rising business and social science professionals. Dr. Walls especially enjoys helping people learn how to live their G.R.E.A.T.E.S.T. Life!

Dr. Walls invites you to visit www.askdrwalls.com.

43052312R00033

Made in the USA
Middletown, DE
29 April 2017